SQUIRRELS

First published 1974 by Oxford University Press, England.
First American publication 1975 by Franklin Watts, Inc.

ISBN 0-531-02754-6
Library of Congress Catalog Card Number: 74–6193

Printed in Austria.

SQUIRRELS

BRIAN WILDSMITH

FRANKLIN WATTS, INC. NEW YORK, N.Y. 1975

It is easy to recognize a squirrel. He is
a furry, small animal with a long, bushy
tail, two strong back legs, two small

front paws, two large tufted ears which stick up, and two big front teeth. He looks happy and mischievous.

In summertime the squirrel's coat is quite
thin. But in wintertime it grows thick and

strong. He seems to have little socks on his
feet and warm fur gloves on his front paws.

Squirrels live in trees.
Sometimes their home is
a hole in an old tree trunk.
Sometimes it is high up
in the treetop in an
abandoned crow's nest.

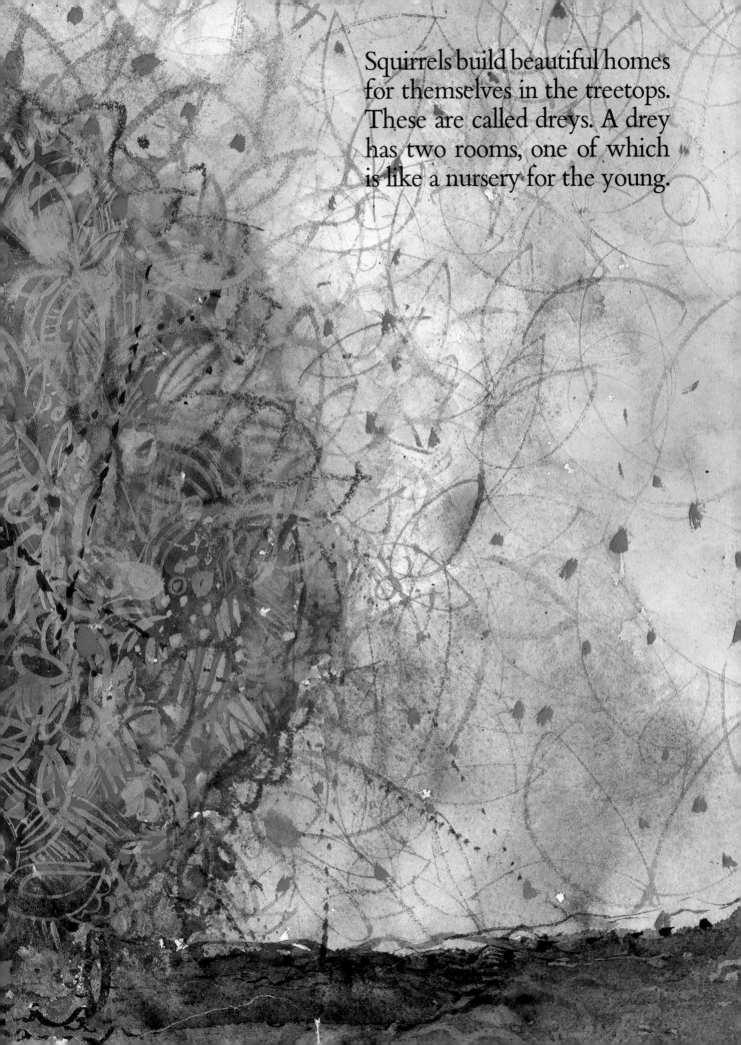

Squirrels build beautiful homes
for themselves in the treetops.
These are called dreys. A drey
has two rooms, one of which
is like a nursery for the young.

Their sharp claws give them a strong
hold on the trunk of a tree, so that they

can scamper both up and
down it with great speed.

Probably no animal in the world uses his tail for so many different purposes. When a squirrel leaps through the air from tree to tree, he can use his tail as a parachute, and it even helps him to change direction.

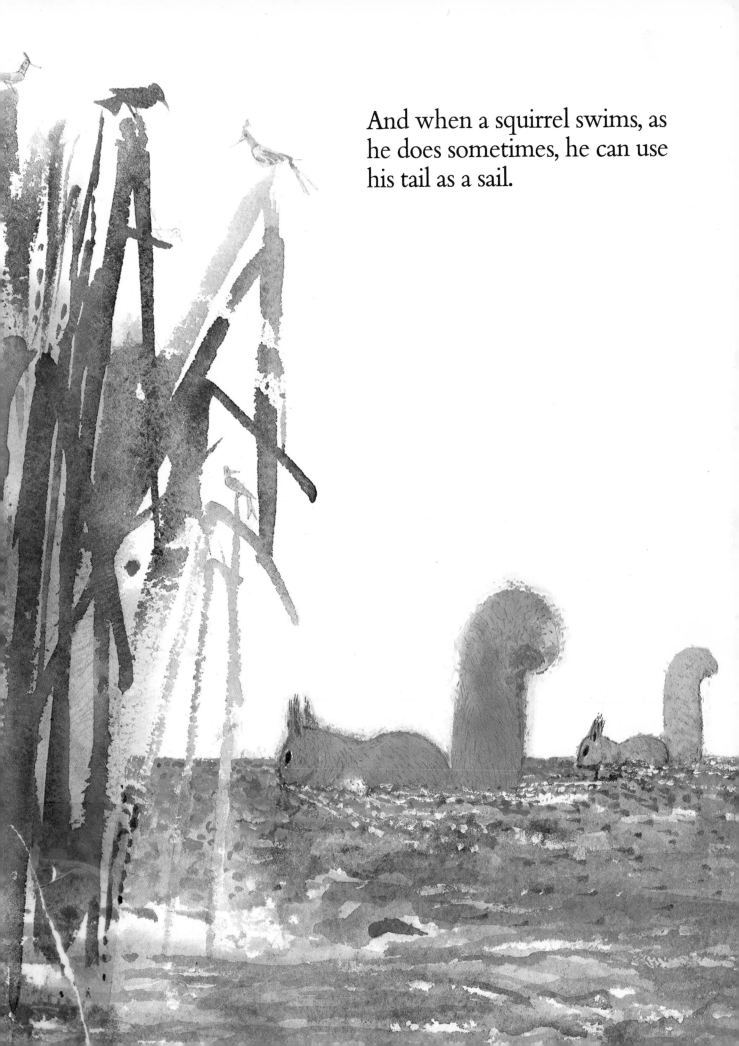

And when a squirrel swims, as he does sometimes, he can use his tail as a sail.

When he scurries along the bough of a tree,

he can use it to balance and guide himself.

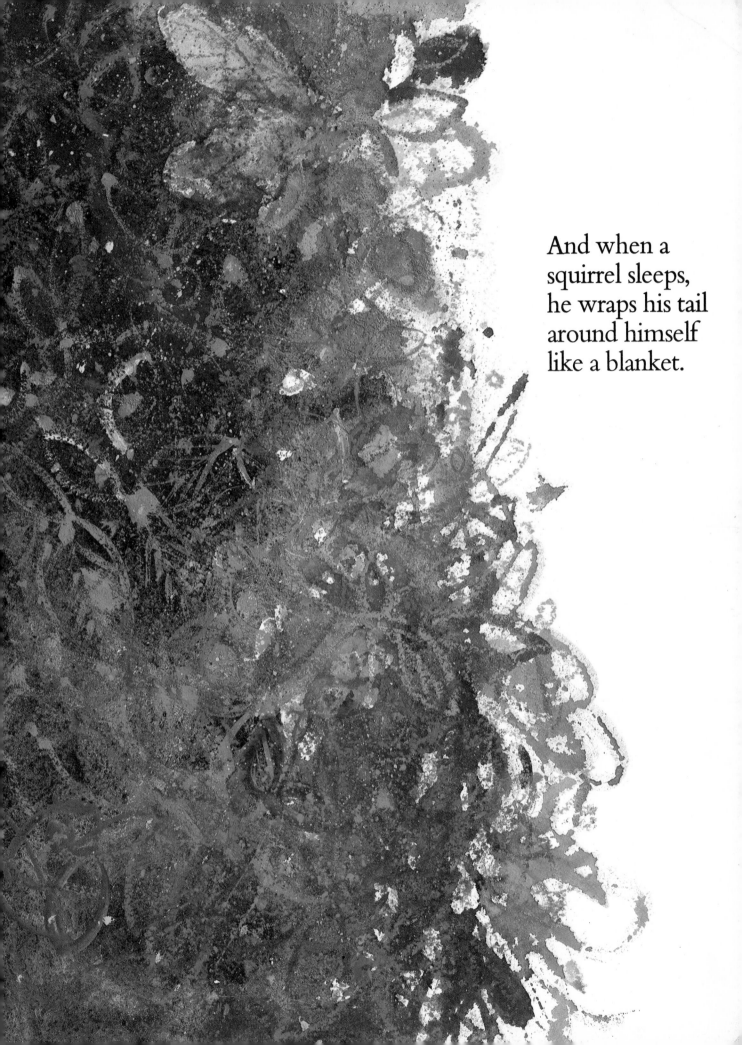

And when a
squirrel sleeps,
he wraps his tail
around himself
like a blanket.

Twice a year – in the spring and at the end of
the summer – the female squirrel has her young,
usually three or four babies at a time. For seven

weeks the mother gives them milk, then they
are ready for a squirrel's favorite foods – nuts,
acorns, wheat, fruit.

In the last
weeks of autumn,
squirrels become
very busy
gathering nuts
and acorns
to eat during the
winter. They
carry them in
their cheek
pouches and hide
them in all kinds
of nooks and
holes around
the trees where
they live.

Squirrels are delightful little creatures, but
they can be destructive. In a garden they

like to pull up new plants, eat bulbs and
even bite the tops off very young trees.

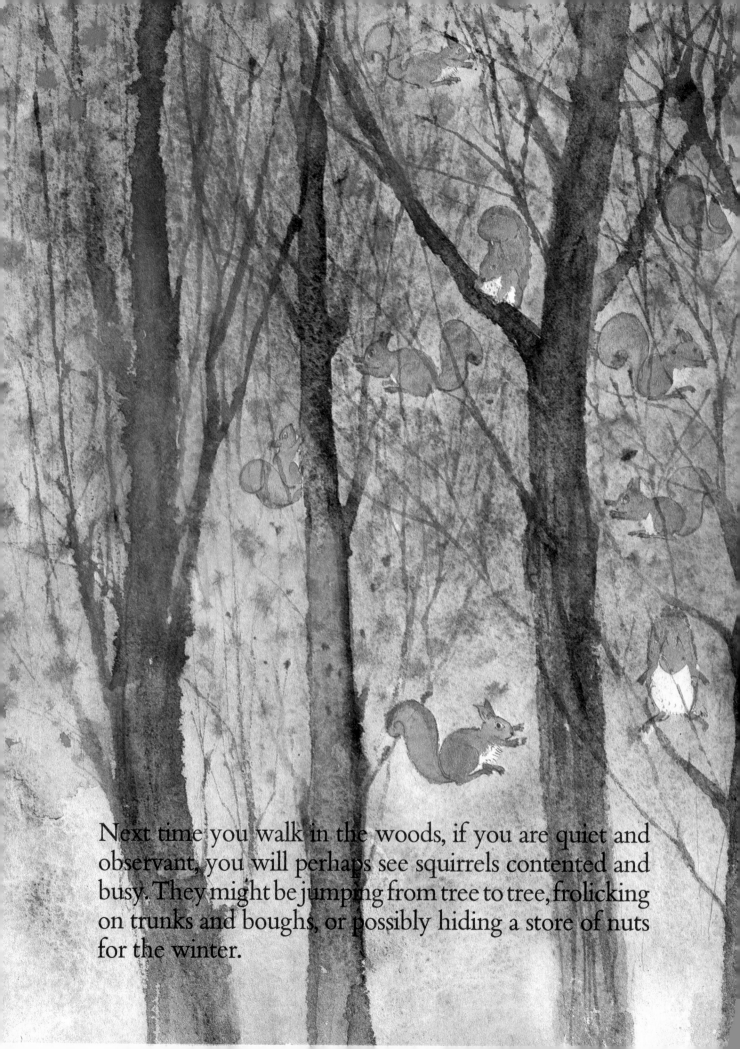

Next time you walk in the woods, if you are quiet and observant, you will perhaps see squirrels contented and busy. They might be jumping from tree to tree, frolicking on trunks and boughs, or possibly hiding a store of nuts for the winter.